Krakow guide 2023

Everything you need to know before plan a Trip to

2023
Krakow

2023 edition

2024 and beyond

Clyde M. King

2023 edition

By **Clyde M. King**

Kindly note that you will be alerted if any of Copyrighted established

Clyde M. King

Table of contents

Title page
Copyright page
Introduction
Index

Chapter 1: Introduction

1.1 Welcome to Krakow
1.2 About this Guide
1.3 How to Use this Book
1.4 Planning Your Trip

Chapter 2: Getting to Know Krakow

2.1 History of Krakow
2.2 Culture and Traditions
2.3 Modern Krakow
2.4 Famous Landmarks

Chapter 3: Top Tourist Attractions

3.1 Wawel Castle and Cathedral
3.2 Rynek Główny (Main Market Square)
3.3 St. Mary's Basilica
3.4 Kazimierz - The Jewish Quarter
3.5 Schindler's Factory Museum
3.6 Wieliczka Salt Mine

Chapter 4: Exploring Krakow's Museums

4.1 National Museum in Krakow

4.2 Cloth Hall (Sukiennice) Gallery of Art

4.3 Manggha Museum of Japanese Art and Technology

4.4 MOCAK - Museum of Contemporary Art in Krakow

Chapter 5: Enjoying Krakow's Nature

5.1 Planty Park

5.2 Kościuszko Mound

5.3 Vistula River Cruise

5.4 Zakrzówek - The Blue Lagoon

Chapter 6: Indulging in Krakow's Cuisine

6.1 Traditional Polish Dishes

6.2 Best Restaurants in Krakow

6.3 Popular Cafes and Street Food

Chapter 7: Shopping in Krakow

7.1 Markets and Souvenirs

7.2 Local Products to Buy

7.3 Shopping Streets and Malls

Chapter 8: Day Trips from Krakow

8.1 Auschwitz-Birkenau Memorial and Museum

8.2 Wieliczka Salt Mine

8.3 Zakopane and the Tatra Mountains

Chapter 9: Insider Tips and Practical Information

9.1 Transportation in Krakow
9.2 Accommodation Options
9.3 Safety and Emergency Contacts
9.4 Useful Phrases in Polish

Conclusion
Thank You for Exploring Krakow
Share Your Experiences
Recommended Further Reading

Welcome to Krakow

Welcome to our travel guide for Krakow! Southern Poland's lovely and ancient city of Krakow is renowned for its extensive cultural history, spectacular architecture, and lively environment. Krakow, one of the oldest and most beautiful cities in the nation, offers tourists a distinctive fusion of heritage and contemporary. Every traveller can find something to do in Krakow, whether they want to take in the local culture, explore historical sites, or indulge in delectable Polish food.

Krakow has a lengthy and intriguing history that dates back to the seventh century. It is still one of Poland's most important cultural hubs despite having formerly been the country's capital. The Old Town, Wawel Castle, and the mediaeval Jagiellonian University are just a some of the city's UNESCO World Heritage Sites. Make sure to check out the many museums and galleries that highlight the city's rich cultural past on your trip to the Main Market Square (Rynek Glowny), one of Europe's biggest mediaeval squares.

Krakow's architecture, which draws inspiration from Gothic, Renaissance, Baroque, and other architectural forms, is a tribute to the city's rich past. Take a stroll around the streets and take in the historic churches and structures that have been so carefully maintained. In addition to offering breathtaking views of the city, the Wawel Royal Castle also has amazing collections of works of art and historical artefacts, making it a must-see site.

Explore Krakow's busy Kazimierz Jewish District, which was formerly an independent municipality and is now a historic Jewish quarter. Synagogues, Jewish museums, and a thriving nightlife can be found in Kazimierz, a city that provides a distinctive fusion of Jewish tradition and modern culture.

Polish food is filling and delectable, and Krakow is a great spot to try some of the traditional specialties. Don't forget to sample classic Polish dishes like bigos (hunter's stew), kielbasa, and pierogi. Also, don't forget to sample some of the renowned obwarzanki bagels from Krakow.

Events & Festivals: Throughout the year, Krakow plays home to a variety of events and festivals. A few of the city's well-known events that provide a distinctive cultural experience include the Christmas Market, the Jewish Culture Festival, and the yearly Krakow Film Festival.

Day travels: Krakow itself has a lot to see and do, but you may also want to explore day travels to adjacent sights. The Wieliczka Salt Mine, the Auschwitz-Birkenau Memorial and Museum, and the Tatra Mountains, which provide wonderful chances for trekking and outdoor experiences, are popular tourist sites.

Local Traditions: Respect Krakow's regional traditions and customs. People may be heard singing traditional songs or participating in a variety of religious and cultural festivities. While touring the city, observe the manners and habits of the locals.

Krakow is a must-see location in Europe because of its fascinating history, beautiful architecture, and welcoming people. Pack your luggage, get ready to explore, and fall in love with this magnificent Polish city's captivating charm!

CHAPTER (ONE)
About this Krakow Travel Guide

This overview of Krakow is meant to serve as a starting point for visitors who want to learn about the city's attractions and most important facts. It attempts to provide readers a broad overview of what to anticipate when seeing Krakow and acts as a jumping-off point for further investigation and preparation.

Krakow's history, culture, architecture, monuments, Kazimierz Jewish Quarter, traditional food, well-known events and festivals, recommended day excursions, and regional customs are all included in the book. It seeks to provide a comprehensive view of the city's experiences and attractions.

It is important to keep in mind that this guide is not a complete resource and could not include the most recent details on certain activities, sights, or changes that may have taken place in Krakow after the knowledge cutoff date in September 2021.

To ensure you have the most up-to-date and accurate information when planning your trip, it is always a good idea to augment the information given here with further research from reputable sources, official tourist websites, and travel forums.

Travel experiences may be individualised, so what appeals to one traveller might not be the same for another. In order to customise your vacation to your own interests and tastes, it is usually advantageous to have a variety of diverse viewpoints and suggestions.

In summary, this book offers details on the history, culture, monuments, and local experiences of Krakow in a clear and informative manner. Its goal is to motivate and aid visitors in getting the most out of their time in this attractive Polish city.

Using This Book in Krakow

Here's how to utilise this Krakow travel guide to its fullest potential:

Read the whole manual: To acquire a broad understanding of Krakow, start by reading the complete guide. You will have a better understanding of the city's main attractions, culture, and experiences as a result.

Highlight Your Interests: As you read, draw attention to the locations and activities that catch your attention. You may concentrate on the attractions that suit your interests since Krakow offers a wide variety of attractions.

Continue Your investigation: Once you've decided the locations you wish to visit, carry out more investigation. Detailed information on each attraction, its hours of operation, admission costs, and any upcoming events or exhibits should be sought out before your visit. To be sure the information is still valid, look for the most recent modifications.

Make an itinerary: Make a basic schedule for your vacation based on your study. Consider the closeness of the locations you wish to see each day while planning your itinerary. You may make the most of your stay in Krakow by doing this.

Plan day trips: Krakow is an excellent place to explore local sights. Plan further excursions, such as going to the Wieliczka Salt Mine or the Auschwitz-Birkenau Memorial and Museum, using the recommended day trips in the book.

Explore the Polish food area and make a list of the meals you want to taste. To sample traditional Polish cuisine, look into nearby eateries or food markets.

Embrace Local Traditions: Get to know the customs and traditions of the area that are covered in the book. To communicate with locals in a more genuine way, respect their culture and customs.

Examine Events: Try to attend any of the aforementioned events or festivals if your vacation falls during one of them. You may fully experience Krakow's lively culture and festivals by attending these events.

Be Open to Discoveries: The handbook is a terrific place to start, but you should also be open to unanticipated discoveries. Explore the streets, engage with the people, and welcome unexpected encounters that the guidebook may not have described.

Verify Current material: Keep in mind that as the material in the guide is based on knowledge as of September 2021, it may not be current. Before your journey, confirm any important information or updates from current sources.

You may design a unique and unforgettable trip to Krakow by using this travel guide as a starting point and adding to it with further study. Enjoy and learn while visiting this captivating Polish city!

Organising Your Travel

To guarantee a seamless and pleasurable experience, meticulous planning and preparation are necessary before travelling to Krakow. The important measures to efficiently planning your vacation are listed below:

Choose Your Travel Dates: Choose the dates that you wish to visit Krakow. Take into account elements like the weather, seasonal activities, and your own schedule. Remember that busy travel times might be more costly and congested.

Once you've decided on your vacation dates, book your tickets to Krakow and make lodging arrangements. Find accommodations that are within your price range and conveniently close to the city's attractions.

Check Poland's visa and entrance requirements according to your nationality by doing some research. Make sure your passport is valid for at least six months after the day you want to travel.

Make a thorough schedule for your trip using the information from the Krakow travel guide and other research. Set aside time for day excursions, big attraction visits, and unstructured exploring.

Establish a budget for your vacation that accounts for the cost of your flights, lodging, meals, transportation, admission fees, and souvenirs. Regarding your expenditures, be reasonable and allot money appropriately.

Invest in Travel Insurance: Protect yourself from unforeseeable situations like trip cancellation, medical problems, or misplaced baggage by investing in travel insurance.

Learn the Fundamental Phrases: Get to know the fundamental Polish expressions. A few local terms may improve your relationships and demonstrate respect for the local culture even if English is often used in tourist regions.

Check the weather forecast for Krakow before you go home and prepare appropriately. Don't forget to pack basics like your passport, batteries, and any other necessary stuff.

Pre-book Tickets and Tours: To avoid lengthy queues and guarantee availability, pre-booking tickets is a good idea if you want to visit famous destinations or take part in guided tours.

Stay Informed: Keep track of the most recent COVID-19 travel warnings and updates, as well as any other possible interruptions. Keep up with any adjustments to the opening and closing times of attractions or to the safety rules.

Notify Your Bank: To prevent any problems using your credit or debit card when travelling overseas, notify your bank of your trip dates.

Consult your physician or a travel health centre to make sure you have the appropriate immunisations and prescriptions for your trip. Observe any health recommendations given by medical professionals.

Bring a Travel Guide or Map: To help you explore Krakow and locate important information on the move, bring a paper or digital travel guidebook or map of the city.

Keep in mind to be adaptable and leave space for spontaneity when travelling. Off the beaten path exploration may lead to some of the finest experiences. Make the most of your time in Krakow and your wonderful journey!

CHAPTER TWO

The past of Krakow

Krakow has a long and extensive history that has origins in antiquity. One of the most historically important cities in Poland, the city has seen varied eras of prosperity, unrest, and cultural blossoming. An outline of Krakow's significant historical turning points is provided below:

Early History: People have lived in the region surrounding modern-day Krakow since the Stone Age. The earliest known village was made on Wawel Hill by a Slavic tribe in the seventh century, when it was fortified. Krakow's early growth was aided by its advantageous placement along trade routes.

Krakow was chosen as the capital of the Polish kingdom in the tenth century. Under the administration of King Bolesaw I Chrobry (Boleslaus the Brave), Krakow was a key player in Poland's unity and territorial expansion.

Krakow was a thriving city throughout the Middle Ages, serving as a significant commerce hub and a centre for the advancement of culture and the arts. The city attracted intellectuals, artists, and merchants, and it was at this time that the famous Wawel Royal Castle and St. Mary's Basilica were being built.

Jagiellonian Period: Krakow saw substantial expansion during the Jagiellonian dynasty's rule in the 14th and 15th centuries. One of Europe's oldest institutions, the University of Krakow, which was established in 1364, was instrumental in the advancement of knowledge and science.

The Polish-Lithuanian Commonwealth, a strong confederation of two nations that spanned from the Baltic to the Black Sea, was headquartered in Krakow in the 16th century. The city achieved economic success and rose to prominence as a centre of Renaissance culture during this time.

Decline and Partition: In the late 18th century, neighbouring nations partitioned Poland on a number of occasions, which caused Krakow's political and economic prominence to gradually wane. The Austrian Empire, which controlled over the area until World War I, annexed the city.

Independence and World War II: In 1918, Poland regained its independence after World War I, and Krakow joined the newly formed Polish state. Nazi Germany seized Krakow during World War II, and the

Jewish community there endured the Holocaust to great devastation.

Post-War Period: Krakow was rebuilt after the war, and great work was put into preserving its historical sites and cultural legacy. The city was a focal point of anti-communist forces throughout the Cold War and played a vital part in Poland's war for independence.

UNESCO World Heritage Site: Recognising Krakow's distinctive historical and cultural value, UNESCO declared the city's historic centre, which includes Wawel Castle and St. Mary's Basilica, as a World Heritage Site in 1978.

Krakow is a thriving city today that embraces modernization while retaining its rich heritage. The city's well-preserved mediaeval architecture, museums, and cultural events may all be explored by visitors to get a sense of its colourful history.

Customs and Culture

Krakow's culture and customs have a rich history that spans many different eras. The intriguing fusion of influences from numerous ages, including the mediaeval, Renaissance, and Baroque eras, can be seen in the city's cultural legacy. Here are some significant facets of Krakow's customs and culture:

Folklore and Festivals: Legends, folk music, and dance are all part of Krakow's rich folklore culture. A man costumed as a Tatar warrior leads a vibrant procession through the streets in the Lajkonik Parade, one of the city's many festivals and celebrations of its cultural history. Another important occasion showcasing Jewish music, art, and gastronomy is the Jewish Culture Festival in Kazimierz.

Religion & Religious Traditions: For many years, Krakow has served as a major centre for religious activity. The area has a long history of Catholicism, and there are several noteworthy churches there, such as St. Mary's Basilica, which is well-known for its famed trumpet call (Hejnal) from the top tower. Many pilgrims go to the Sanctuary of Divine Mercy in the Agiewniki neighbourhood, which is dedicated to Saint Faustina Kowalska, the Divine Mercy apostle.

Polish food is very important to Krakow culture, and the residents take great pleasure in their traditional delicacies. A common delicacy is pierogi (dumplings) filled with a variety of ingredients, including as potatoes, cheese, or meat. In addition, Krakow is well known for its kielbasa (Polish sausage) and obwarzanki, a sort of bagel.

Traditional Dance and Music: Krakow continues to value traditional Polish dance and music. Folk music and dances are performed live for audience members at a variety of locations and during festivals. Numerous folk groups in the city support and maintain traditional forms of expression.

Craftsmanship and artisan traditions have a long history in Krakow, which boasts a thriving cultural sector. The city provides a wide variety of creative expressions, from antique wood carvings and needlework to modern art galleries.

Language and Protocol: The official language of Krakow is Polish. Polish language proficiency may improve your contacts with people and demonstrate respect for their culture. Polish etiquette demands politeness and consideration for senior citizens.

Historical Architecture: The Gothic, Renaissance, and Baroque architectural styles seen in Krakow represent the city's rich cultural legacy. Two outstanding examples of the city's architectural splendour are the ancient Old Town and Wawel Castle.

Socialising and Hospitality: Poles are renowned for their friendly hospitality. It's normal to provide a modest present for the host upon being asked to someone's house, such as flowers or chocolates. Meals and get-togethers with friends and family are frequent focal points of social interaction.

Traditions and customs: Krakow maintains several traditions, such as the breaking of the opatek (Christmas wafer) at the supper on Christmas Eve, when well wishes are exchanged for the next year. Easter festivities are also important, with customary food blessings and unique processions.

The custom of creating Christmas crib nativity scenes and the craft of manufacturing traditional paper cut-outs (wycinanki) are among the cultural practises that Poland has placed on UNESCO's list of intangible cultural assets.

Any trip to Krakow must include taking in the local culture and customs. Adopt the traditions of the area, participate in events, and experience Krakow's distinctive ambiance for yourself.

Current Krakow

In addition to embracing modernity, Krakow, a city with a rich historical and cultural history, has grown into a flourishing and vibrant metropolitan hub. Here are a few features of contemporary Krakow:

Krakow is a hub for education and innovation since it is home to a number of universities and research facilities. One of the world's oldest institutions, the Jagiellonian University was established in 1364 and now plays a significant part in fostering intellectual brilliance.

Technology and startups: The tech environment in Krakow is expanding, with several startups and IT firms setting up shop there. Co-working establishments, incubators, and tech centres have encouraged creativity and the spirit of entrepreneurship.

Culture & Contemporary Art: The city is home to a bustling contemporary art scene, with several galleries and exhibition halls showing the creations of both national and foreign artists. Notable cultural institutions include the Manggha Museum of Japanese Art and

Technology and the MOCAK (Museum of Contemporary Art in Krakow).

Modern Architecture: Krakow is known for its ancient buildings, but it has also benefited from the growth of more contemporary structures and infrastructure. New office buildings, retail malls and apartment structures merge nicely with the city's historic beauty.

Krakow's culinary culture has grown to include a variety of eateries, cafés, and pubs serving cuisines from across the world and providing hip eating experiences. Despite the continued popularity of traditional Polish cuisine, you can also discover a variety of contemporary culinary ideas.

Festivals & Events: Krakow also holds a number of contemporary events and cultural festivals that appeal to a range of interests, in addition to its historical festivals. Visitors from all around the globe attend international events, music festivals, and film festivals.

Recreational activities and green places are valued in contemporary Krakow. The Old Town is encircled by the Planty Park, which provides a lovely setting for leisurely strolls and relaxation. Outdoor sports are also quite popular along the banks of the Vistula River.

Environment and Sustainability: The city has made attempts to promote environmental awareness. Krakow's dedication to becoming an environmentally aware city is shown by its measures for cleaner public transit, bicycle-friendly routes, and green projects.

tourist and hospitality: Krakow's tourist sector has expanded significantly, offering a variety of lodging alternatives, from five-star resort hotels to low-cost hostels. Travellers from all over the globe are drawn to the city by its friendly attitude and thriving cultural scene.

Infrastructure and Connectivity: Krakow has first-rate transport options, including an international airport, well-connected public transit, and a system of highways that make it easy to get throughout the city and to other areas.

Krakow as it is now is the ideal fusion of its historical past with modern conveniences and advancements. All sorts of travellers find the city to be an interesting destination since they may explore its fascinating history while taking use of current metropolitan comforts.

Renowned landmarks

Numerous well-known sites in Krakow serve as a testament to the city's rich heritage and exquisite architecture. Here are some of the city's must-see landmarks:

Wawel Castle: This famous fortress is perched atop Wawel Hill and represents Krakow's regal heritage. It is a fine example of Renaissance and Gothic architecture and was the home of Polish kings and queens. The Wawel Cathedral, where Polish kings and queens were crowned and interred, is part of the castle complex.

One of Krakow's most recognisable monuments is St. Mary's Basilica, which is situated in the Main Market Square (Rynek Glowny). The city's skyline is dominated by its twin towers. The basilica's interior is noted for its magnificent altar, vibrant stained glass windows, and distinctive trumpet call (Hejnal), which is played from one of the towers every hour.

The Cloth Hall (Sukiennice), a historic market hall from the Renaissance period, is located in the Main Market Square. Since it has long been a centre of trade and business, it still includes gift stores and tiny marketplaces where people may purchase authentic Polish handicrafts.

Jewish District of Kazimierz: Known for its extensive Jewish history, Kazimierz is a bustling neighbourhood with cobblestone lanes, old synagogues, and quaint cafés. It serves as a reminder of the once-vibrant Jewish population that previously called Krakow home.

The Wieliczka Salt Mine is a UNESCO World Heritage Site and a distinctive attraction that is just a short drive from Krakow. Visitors are welcome to visit the chapels, sculptures, and subterranean chambers made completely of salt by the mine's former employees.

Planty Park is a beautiful green belt that encircles the famous Old Town and provides a tranquil escape from the busy metropolis. It is a well-liked location for relaxing walks.

Florian's Gate is a well-preserved Gothic tower and a significant historical site. It was one of the original entrances to the mediaeval city.

The Krakow Barbican A fortified outpost from the fifteenth century is called Barbican. One of the few surviving pieces of the city's ancient defences may be found there.

Oskar Schindler's old enamel factory, made famous by the film "Schindler's List," is now home to the Museum of Contemporary Art in Krakow (MOCAK), which also has a permanent exhibition on the Holocaust and Krakow's history during World War II.

St. Florian's Church is a gorgeous example of mediaeval architecture that stands just outside the city walls. It is dedicated to St. Florian, the patron saint of firemen, and is located there.

Along with many other attractions, these sites provide tourists a window into Krakow's famous history and dynamic present. They add to the city's allure. Krakow is a place rich in historical and cultural gems since each landmark has an own history to tell.

CHAPTER (THREE)

Castle and Cathedral of Wawel

Two of Krakow, Poland's most recognisable and historically important monuments are the Wawel Castle and Cathedral. They are all located on Wawel Hill, which has a view of the Vistula River, and together they make up a magnificent complex that honours Poland's former regal era.

Castle Wawel:

History: Wawel Castle was home to Polish monarchs and queens for many years. Its history dates back to the 11th century. It was the centre of Polish politics and culture and was the scene of many important historical occurrences.

Romanesque, Gothic, Renaissance, and Baroque architectural elements are used in the design of the castle. The castle experienced various additions and improvements throughout the years, giving it its current spectacular aspect.

Outer Courtyard, the castle's main courtyard, is open to the public and offers breathtaking views of the building's many wings and turrets.

State Rooms: The sumptuous State Rooms, which include the Royal Apartments and the Senate Hall and are furnished with elaborate décor and historical artefacts, are open to visitors.

Wawel Dragon: A statue of the Wawel Dragon, a fabled being connected to Krakow's mythology, may be found close to the castle. Legend has it that Krakus, the city's hero, killed the dragon.

The Royal Archcathedral Basilica of Saints Stanislaus and Wenceslaus, or Wawel Cathedral:

History: For centuries, Polish monarchs and queens were crowned and buried in Wawel Cathedral, one of Poland's most revered ecclesiastical landmarks. It serves as the archbishop of Krakow's residence as well.

Architecture: The cathedral's architecture combines many different design eras, with Gothic and Renaissance characteristics predominating in the contemporary building. It dominates the city's skyline with its tall spires and elaborate exterior.

Sigismund Bell: The cathedral's Sigismund Bell, one of Poland's biggest bells, is rung on significant days and occasions.

Crypts and Chapels: Inside the cathedral, guests may tour the crypts holding the graves of prominent historical individuals and Polish kings. Among the cathedral's prominent chapels are the Silver Bell Chapel, the Zygmunt Chapel, and the Holy Cross Chapel.

Saint Stanislaus: The remains of St. Stanislaus, the patron saint of Poland, whose martyrdom helped the country become Christian, are kept in the cathedral.

Polish culture and history are inextricably linked to the Wawel Castle and Cathedral, whose magnificence continues to draw tourists from all over the globe. For visitors want to fully experience Krakow's rich history and architectural splendour, the complex is a must-visit location.

The Main Market Square, Rynek Gówny

Rynek Gówny, sometimes referred to as the Main Market plaza, is the biggest mediaeval plaza in Europe and the centre of Krakow's historic Old Town. It serves as a focal point for both residents and visitors and is a hive of activity. The plaza is a bright and exciting location since it is surrounded by stunning architecture, significant monuments, and busy eateries. The Main Market Square's main attributes and attractions are listed below:

Size & Layout: Rynek Gówny is a rectangular square with a floor size of around 40,000 square metres (430,000 square feet). On each side, it is about 200 metres (656 feet) long.

The famous Cloth Hall (Sukiennice), a structure from the Renaissance period, is located in the middle of the plaza. It is a former marketplace where traders previously exchanged commodities including textiles, spices, and other products. Today, the Cloth Hall is home to kiosks offering traditional Polish crafts and souvenir businesses.

One of Krakow's most spectacular churches, St. Mary's Basilica (Koció Mariacki), is located at the northern end of the Main Market Square. The basilica is a must-see destination due to its magnificent Gothic architecture and vibrant interiors. Additionally, visitors may climb the tower for sweeping views of the plaza.

Town Hall Tower: The Town Hall Tower (Wiea ratuszowa) is a piece of the demolished 19th-century Town Hall. Visitors may climb the tower, which is located on the square's eastern edge, for beautiful views of the Old Town.

Festivals & Events: To honour Polish culture and customs, the Main Market Square stages a number of festivals, events, and concerts throughout the year.

Horse-Drawn Carriages: The area is often lined with vibrant horse-drawn carriages that offer travellers relaxing and romantic rides.

Restaurants & cafés: There are several dining establishments, cafés, and outdoor terraces all around the Main Market Square. It's the perfect place to unwind with a meal or a drink and take in the bustling ambiance.

Market booths: In addition to the Cloth Hall, there are various market booths and street sellers selling crafts, refreshments, and souvenirs.

Christmas Market: Over the course of the holiday season, the Main Market Square is transformed into a lovely Christmas Market with wooden kiosks offering presents, seasonal décor, and traditional Christmas fare.

Anyone visiting Krakow should stop at the Main Market Square, a lively and significant meeting spot that showcases the city's rich cultural past. The many tourist attractions, museums, and historical sites that surround this gorgeous area are all easily accessible from here.

Sacred Heart Basilica

One of the most well-known and stunning cathedrals in Krakow, Poland, is St. Mary's Basilica, or Koció Mariacki. It is a notable representation of the city's religious and architectural legacy and is situated on the northern side of the Main Market Square (Rynek Góówny). Here are some of St. Mary's Basilica's salient characteristics and details:

St. Mary's Basilica is a magnificent example of Gothic style in architecture. One of Krakow's most recognisable sights is its unusual twin towers, which have differing heights and architectural styles. Aproximate heights of the two towers are 69 metres (226 feet) and 81 metres (265 feet), respectively.

Exterior: The St. Mary's Basilica's exterior is decorated with exquisite tracery, complex stone carvings, and pointed arches that are characteristic of the Gothic architectural style. Numerous sculptures, including depictions of saints and biblical characters, cover the outside.

Interior: St. Mary's Basilica's interior is similarly remarkable. The breathtakingly high vaulted ceilings, vibrant stained glass windows, and elaborate altars astound visitors. The basilica is home to several priceless works of art, religious artefacts, and historical artefacts.

The exquisite wooden altarpiece known as the High Altar or the Altarpiece of Veit Stoss (Otarz Wita Stwosza) is one of the basilica's centrepieces. It is a masterwork of late Gothic art and was carved by the German artist Veit Stoss. It features scenes from the life of the Virgin Mary and the Passion of Christ.

The Hejnal, a trumpet signal blown from the upper tower, is one of the distinctive customs connected to St. Mary's Basilica. Every hour, the Hejnal is performed, and it ends suddenly to remember a famous incident in which the bugler was shot in the neck while alerting the city to an approaching Mongol invasion.

Mass & Worship: St. Mary's Basilica is a bustling house of prayer, holding daily Masses for both residents and tourists. The church is well-known for its exquisite choral performances and sacred rituals.

St. Mary's Basilica is accessible to guests throughout the year. During the permitted visiting hours, guests are welcome to tour the church and take in its splendour.

View from the Tower: A journey to the higher tower is available for those who want to take in expansive views of Krakow. The views from the tower of the Main Market Square and the surrounding area are stunning.

In addition to being a work of art, St. Mary's Basilica is an important spiritual and cultural monument in Krakow. It is a must-see location for tourists interested in learning about the city's rich history due to its historical relevance, gorgeous architecture, and religious significance.

The Jewish Quarter in Kazimierz

In Krakow, Poland, a historic district with a rich and intriguing Jewish history is known as Kazimierz, also known as the Jewish Quarter. It is close to the Old Town and has grown to be a well-liked stop for tourists interested in learning about the Jewish heritage, culture, and creative life of the city. Here are some of Kazimierz's salient characteristics and highlights:

Jewish History: King Casimir III founded Kazimierz as a distinct town in the 14th century, and throughout the years, it developed into a thriving hub of Jewish culture and activity. Kazimierz has a long and illustrious Jewish history.

Synagogues: There are several old synagogues in Kazimierz, each with a distinctive architectural design and historical value. The Old Synagogue (Stara Synagoga), Remuh Synagogue, and High Synagogue are a few of the noteworthy synagogues.

Jewish Culture: The area's winding alleyways, lovely courtyards, and structures that pay homage to the Jewish community's earlier days give off a distinctly Jewish vibe.

Jewish Quarter Film Festival: Held annually in Kazimierz, the Jewish Culture Festival honours Jewish customs via music, art, and film. Local and foreign artists and tourists are drawn there.

Szeroka Street: This bustling thoroughfare in Kazimierz is famous for its eateries and outdoor cafés. Both residents and visitors frequent this famous location to take in the energetic surroundings.

Jewish history and memory of Jewish life in Poland and the Galicia area are preserved at the Galicia Jewish Museum. It has displays, images, and artefacts that provide insights into Jewish tradition and culture.

Street Art and Murals: Kazimierz has developed into a centre for street art and murals, with a number of gifted painters putting their imprint on the area's walls, bringing a contemporary and imaginative touch to the neighborhood's old-world surroundings.

Festivals & Events: To further enhance its thriving cultural scene, Kazimierz offers a variety of cultural events, including as music festivals, art exhibits, and Jewish holiday celebrations.

Jewish cemetery: The Remuh Cemetery and the New Jewish Cemetery are the two Jewish cemetery in Kazimierz. The graves of noteworthy Jewish personalities are located in these cemeteries, which are important historical locations.

Locations for Schindler's List: Several sequences from the film "Schindler's List" were shot in Kazimierz, especially along Szeroka Street and Plac Nowy. Significant changes have been made to the neighborhood's appeal as a travel destination as a result of the movie.

Today, Kazimierz is a fascinating area that honours both its Jewish past and its contemporary creative vitality. Exploring Krakow's ancient synagogues, museums, and

distinctive ambiance will give visitors a deeper
understanding of Polish Jewish history and culture.

Museum at Schindler's Factory

The Schindler's Factory Museum is an important
historical and cultural landmark in Krakow, Poland. Its
official name is the Museum of Contemporary Art in
Krakow (MOCAK). The museum is housed in the
former administrative building of Oskar Schindler's
enamel factory, which rose to fame thanks to Steven
Spielberg's movie 'Schindler's List'. The Schindler's
Factory Museum offers a thorough and immersive
experience, illuminating the historical events
surrounding the Holocaust and Krakow during World
War II. Here are some key features and highlights of the
museum:

History: The museum is devoted to portraying the tale of
Oskar Schindler, a German manufacturer who employed
more than a thousand Jewish workers at his factory and
therefore saved their lives during the Holocaust. The
exhibit also discusses Krakow's larger historical setting
during the Nazi period.

exhibits: The museum is home to a number of
thought-provoking exhibits that portray the history and

experiences of the conflict via the use of multimedia, artefacts, documents, and works of art. It addresses issues including life in the Jewish ghetto, living under occupation, and Krakow's Jewish population's destiny.

Permanent display: The "Krakow Under Nazi Occupation 1939–1945" permanent display offers a thorough overview of the city's history during that time. It uses interactive displays, images, and first-person stories to tell a powerful and poignant story.

Temporary exhibits: In addition to the permanent display, the museum hosts a variety of contemporary art exhibits that change often and frequently explore themes of conflict, remembrance, and societal concerns.

The museum is housed in the old administrative building of Schindler's enamel factory, contributing to its authenticity and historical value.

Multimedia Experience: To engage visitors and make historical events more concrete, the museum makes use of multimedia installations, video displays, and interactive features.

Educational Programmes: To encourage comprehension and critical thought on the Holocaust and World War II, the museum provides educational programmes for classrooms and visitors of all ages.

The museum contains a bookshop where visitors may discover literature about the Holocaust and Krakow's history. It also has a café. In addition, there is a café where visitors may unwind and reflect after visiting the museum.

The Schindler's Factory Museum honours Oskar Schindler's valiant deeds and the history of the Holocaust in a very poignant and instructive way. In addition to serving as a sobering reminder of past crimes, it also acts as a warning against intolerance and prejudice in the present and the future. The complexity of human behaviour during times of war and the fortitude of people who overcame such trials are two important lessons that visitors to the museum learn.

Salt Mine of Wieliczka

One of Poland's most well-known and intriguing tourist destinations is the Wieliczka Salt Mine, which is situated in the Polish town of Wieliczka close to Krakow. A unique subterranean structure that provides visitors with a view into the history of salt mining and the amazing creativity of the miners, it is a UNESCO World Heritage

Site. Here are some of the Wieliczka Salt Mine's salient characteristics and highlights:

History: The Wieliczka Salt Mine is one of the oldest salt mines in the world that has been continually in operation, with a history that dates back to the 13th century. The mine no longer produces salt, but it is still a well-liked tourist site.

Approximately 327 metres (1,073 feet) of subterranean space is occupied by the mine's enormous network of tunnels, chambers, and passages. A total of 2.5 kilometres (1.6 miles) of well-maintained passageways are open to visitors.

The collection of beautiful salt statues and sculptures made by the workers themselves is the mine's most stunning feature, along with the chapels. Numerous chapels, shrines, and sculptures constructed completely of salt are examples of the miners' creative skill.

The church of St. Kinga, also known as Kaplica Witej Kingi, is a breathtaking subterranean church that was totally carved out of salt. It is one of the mine's attractions. It's renowned for its exquisite salt chandeliers and fine salt reliefs.

Salt Lakes: The Wieliczka Salt Mine also has a number of subterranean salt lakes, which heightens the mystery of the underground realm.

Healing Properties: It is reported that the air within the salt mine has healing qualities and is good for respiratory health. As a consequence, people seeking respite from respiratory ailments have been drawn to the mine's microclimate.

Visitors may take guided tours of the salt mine where they can explore several chambers, discover the history of salt mining, and take in the exquisite salt sculptures and works of art.

Special Occasions: The mine accommodates a variety of events, such as concerts, art exhibits, and even wedding ceremonies, making it a distinctive and memorable location for such events.

heritage of the Miners: The Wieliczka salt miner's heritage and folklore are rich, and the distinctive subterranean artwork and chapels they built honour their labour and artistry.

The Wieliczka Salt Mine is a fascinating excursion into the earth's interior that demonstrates human inventiveness and the historical importance of salt mining. Due to the mine's unique blend of untouched natural beauty and man-made marvels, it is a popular tourist site and a symbol of Poland's industrial and cultural legacy.

CHAPTER FOUR

Krakow National Museum

One of Poland's most significant and well-known cultural institutions is the National Museum in Krakow (Muzeum Narodowe w Krakowie). A vast array of works of art, historical artefacts, and cultural treasures are kept in its network of many branches and museums. Here are some of the National Museum in Krakow's salient characteristics and highlights:

Main Building: The National Museum's main structure is situated in Krakow at Aleja 3 Maja. It is a stunning example of 19th-century architecture and is home to a huge collection of artwork and historical displays.

Branches: The Krakow National Museum has a number of locations across the city. The Cloth Hall Gallery, the Czartoryski Museum and Library, the Emeryk Hutten-Czapski Museum, and the Gallery of 19th-Century Polish Art in the Sukiennice (Cloth Hall) are a few of the more noteworthy outposts.

Art holdings: From mediaeval to contemporary art, the museum's art holdings include pieces from a variety of time periods and aesthetic movements. With paintings and sculptures created by notable Polish painters of the 19th century, the Gallery of 19th-Century Polish Art is especially significant.

Historical and archaeological exhibitions are also available in the National Museum, where artefacts from various periods in Polish history are on show.

Foreign Art Collection: The museum's significant foreign art collection includes European paintings, sculptures, and decorative arts in addition to its collection of Polish artwork.

The National Museum often presents temporary exhibits that include works by contemporary artists, unique themed presentations, and artworks that have been lent from other institutions.

Educational Programmes: The museum provides workshops, educational programmes, and tours for visitors of all ages, making it a fun and instructive experience for kids and families.

Preservation of Poland's cultural legacy is ensured by the National Museum's commitment to the conservation and restoration of artworks and cultural artefacts.

Cultural Events: To further enhance visitor experiences and advance art and culture in the community, the museum sponsors a number of cultural events, talks, and concerts.

Visitors may get a greater knowledge of Poland's cultural history by visiting the National Museum in Krakow, which is a treasure mine of the country's creative and historical past. A trip to the National Museum provides a thorough overview of Poland's aesthetic and cultural accomplishments throughout the ages, whether you are interested in history, art, or archaeology.

Sukiennice Cloth Hall Art Gallery

The Cloth Hall, often referred to as Sukiennice in Polish, is a historic structure that can be seen in Krakow's Main Market Square (Rynek Gówny). It has been a vital part of the city's business and cultural life and is an important architectural landmark. One of the divisions of the Krakow National Museum is housed in the Cloth Hall: the Gallery of Polish Art from the Nineteenth Century. The Cloth Hall and the Gallery of Polish Art from the Nineteenth Century include the following salient qualities and highlights:

History: The Renaissance era is when the Cloth Hall first appeared. It was first constructed in the 13th century, but was subsequently burned down and rebuilt in the 16th century in the present Renaissance style. Through the ages, it has functioned as a hub for trade and business, particularly in textiles.

Architecture: The Cloth Hall is an architectural marvel with a magnificent façade embellished with ornamental features and sculptures and a lengthy arcade with pointed arches on its ground level. It is a popular destination for both residents and tourists due to its prominent placement in the Main Market Square.

Polish Art Gallery from the Nineteenth Century: The Cloth Hall's top level is home to the Polish Art Gallery from the Nineteenth Century. The collection of the gallery is devoted to highlighting the creative accomplishments of Polish painters during the 19th century, a time of notable cultural and artistic development in Poland.

Art Collection: The collection consists of pieces from many creative movements, including Symbolism, Romanticism, and Realism. Famous Polish painters from that time have left behind paintings, sculptures, and other works of art for visitors to enjoy.

Masterpieces: Works by painters like Jan Matejko, Jacek Malczewski, Henryk Siemiradzki, and many others who were significant in influencing Polish art throughout the 19th century are among the masterpieces on show at the museum.

The Gallery of 19th-Century Polish Art also conducts temporary exhibits and themed presentations that provide a wider perspective on the time period and its artists, in addition to its permanent collection.

Accessibility: During the museum's regular business hours, guests may browse the art collection in the Cloth Hall and the Gallery of 19th-Century Polish Art.

Environment: Because the Cloth Hall is situated on the Main Market plaza, guests may explore other local landmarks including St. Mary's Basilica, Town Hall Tower, and the lively ambiance of the plaza.

Visitors get a wonderful chance to immerse themselves in Poland's cultural legacy by visiting the Cloth Hall and the Gallery of 19th-Century Polish Art, which exhibits the brilliance and originality of Polish painters throughout the 19th century. The Cloth Hall is a must-visit location for art lovers and history buffs alike because of its historical importance, gorgeous architecture, and excellent paintings.

Japanese art and technology museum Manggha

The Muzeum Sztuki i Techniki Japoskiej Manggha, often known as the Manggha Museum of Japanese Art and Technology, is a distinctive cultural establishment situated in Krakow, Poland. It acts as a link between Poland and Japan and is committed to promoting Japanese art, culture, and technology. The name "Manggha" for the museum is drawn from Feliks Jasieski, a well-known Polish painter and art historian who had a keen interest in Japanese art. The Manggha Museum's main attributes and highlights are listed below:

The Manggha Museum was established in 1994 and is housed in a contemporary structure created by the Japanese architect Arata Isozaki on the banks of the Vistula River in Krakow.

The primary emphasis of the museum is on Japanese art, culture, and customs. It has a large collection of Japanese paintings, prints, pottery, textiles, and other traditional and modern works of art.

Temporary Exhibitions: The Manggha Museum often offers transient displays that highlight many facets of

Japanese history, culture, and technology. These exhibits often include pieces on loan from museums in Japan and other countries.

Tea House: The museum contains a traditional Japanese tea house (chashitsu), where guests may participate in a traditional tea ceremony led by trained Japanese tea masters.

Workshops & Events: To foster a knowledge of Japanese art, history, and traditions, the museum hosts educational workshops, lectures, film screenings, and cultural events.

Japanese Garden: The area around the museum has a tranquil Japanese garden created to mimic the feel of a traditional Japanese environment and provide tourists a tranquil refuge.

Technology & Innovation: The Manggha Museum, in addition to emphasising art and culture, also features technical developments and breakthroughs from Japan, reflecting the nation's status as a pioneer in this field.

Manggha Library: The museum's library has a selection of books and articles about Japanese art, culture, and history, making it a useful tool for aficionados and scholars.

Cultural interaction: The Manggha Museum is essential in creating mutual understanding and respect for one another's cultural heritages through encouraging cultural interaction between Poland and Japan.

For tourists interested in Japanese culture, art, and technical breakthroughs, the Manggha Museum of Japanese Art and Technology provides an engaging and educational experience. It is a notable cultural institution in Krakow because of its commitment to preserving and promoting the beauty of Japanese customs and because it serves as a bridge between two cultures.

Krakow's MOCAK, or Museum of Contemporary Art

The MOCAK, commonly referred to as the Museum of Contemporary Art in Krakow (Muzeum Sztuki Wspóczesnej w Krakowie MOCAK), is a well-known cultural centre in Krakow, Poland, that specialises in contemporary art. It displays a varied selection of current and modern artworks by Polish and foreign artists, spanning many different creative fields and genres. Here are some of the MOCAK - Museum of Contemporary Art in Krakow's salient qualities and highlights:

Location and building design: The museum is housed in a cutting-edge structure with outstanding architectural features that was created by renowned Polish architect Claudio Nardi and is situated in Krakow's Podgórze neighbourhood. The building's design provides a cutting-edge and modern area for art while enhancing the neighborhood's traditional architecture.

A variety of modern works, including paintings, sculptures, installations, photos, films, and multimedia art, are included in the MOCAK's permanent collection. Modern art from the latter half of the 20th century to the present is the collection's primary emphasis.

Polish and Foreign Artists: The museum exhibits artwork by both Polish and foreign artists, offering a venue for creative expression and cross-cultural interaction.

Temporary exhibits: The MOCAK also offers recurring temporary exhibits that highlight the most recent advancements and trends in contemporary art, in addition to its permanent collection. These shows often include both established artists and up-and-coming artists.

For visitors of all ages, the MOCAK offers seminars, lectures, guided tours, and interactive activities as part of its commitment to art education and outreach programmes. With the help of these initiatives, the general public is meant to get more involved and develop a greater appreciation for modern art.

Special Projects and Events: The museum often hosts special projects, plays, film screenings, and other events that investigate the connections between art and many academic fields and facets of contemporary life.

Cultural Initiatives: The MOCAK actively engages with various cultural organisations, galleries, and institutions both domestically and internationally, taking part in cultural initiatives and collaborative projects.

Library and Archive: For academics, students, and art lovers interested in contemporary art and its different facets, the museum's library and archive provide useful resources.

After seeing the art displays, guests may unwind and think after visiting the museum's café and bookshop.

An energetic and progressive organisation that honours the variety and originality of contemporary art is Krakow's MOCAK - Museum of Contemporary Art. Visitors looking to immerse themselves in the always changing landscape of contemporary creative expression will find it to be a rewarding experience. Anyone interested in discovering the leading edge of current creative endeavours must visit the museum because of its dedication to art education and cultural discussion.

CHAPTER (FIVE)
Park Planty

A verdant green belt known as Planty Park or Planty Gardens encircles Krakow's historic district in Poland. It offers inhabitants and visitors alike a tranquil and quiet retreat from the busy metropolis by acting as a green oasis within it. Here are some of Planty Park's main characteristics and highlights:

After the city's mediaeval defence walls were torn down in the early 19th century, Planty Park was built. To replace the fortifications and establish a green area for the delight of Krakow's citizens, the park was built.

Layout: The park, which has a total size of around 21.5 hectares (53 acres), forms a ring around the Old Town. It is separated into many portions, each of which has an own personality and set of characteristics, and it spans a distance of around 4 km (2.5 miles).

Planty Park is attractively designed, with tree-lined pathways, flowerbeds, lawns, and ornamental plants. The layout of the park features a number of little squares, fountains, and seats for people to sit on and unwind.

Walking and Cycling trails: The park is a well-liked location for outdoor activities and leisurely strolls since it is crisscrossed by walking and cycling trails.

Monuments & Statues: Planty Park is filled with statues, memorials, and monuments honouring important historical persons and occasions.

Seasonal Attractions: The park erupts with brilliant foliage and colourful blossoms throughout the spring and summer, making for a stunning backdrop for picnics and outdoor gatherings. The park is more charming in the fall because of the changing foliage.

Cultural Events: To enhance its lively ambiance, Planty Park periodically holds cultural events, outdoor concerts, and open-air exhibits.

Historic Sites: The park is close to a number of Krakow's historical sites, enabling tourists to see the city's architectural gems while taking in the scenery.

Recreation & Relaxation: Planty Park offers a wonderful setting for leisure activities including reading, people-watching, and taking in the outdoors. It is a popular location for residents to relax and take in Krakow's natural beauty.

The park is readily accessible from several locations across the city, making it a popular attraction for both visitors and locals.

Loved for its beautiful fusion of history and nature, Planty Park is a well-known feature of Krakow's metropolitan setting. It is a crucial part of Krakow's charm and character and offers a nice break from the hectic city streets. Planty Park is a great place for people of all ages to go if they want to take a leisurely stroll, have some time to think, or just enjoy the greenery of the city.

Mound of Kociuszko

The Kociuszko Mound, or Kopiec Kociuszki as it is called in Polish, is a historically significant mound that can be seen near Krakow, Poland. Although there are several mounds in the region, the Kociuszko Mound is the most well-known and prominent one. Tadeusz Kociuszko, a national hero and military commander who battled for Poland's independence and freedom in the 18th century, is remembered by the mound, which was built in his honour. The Kociuszko Mound's main characteristics and highlights are listed below:

History and Construction: Tadeusz Kociuszko was respected for his participation in the American Revolutionary War and his attempts to protect Poland throughout different uprisings. The Kociuszko Mound was built between 1820 and 1823 to honour his life and accomplishments.

Location: The mound is located on the Krakus Mound, an old prehistoric mound on Krakus Hill in the city of Krakow.

The Kociuszko Mound is a man-made mound that has a conical form. It is also rather tall. It has a diameter of around 90 metres (295 feet) and rises to a height of about 34 metres (112 feet). Its shape, which is evocative of ancient burial mounds, represents Kociuszko's enduring legacy.

Panoramic vistas: The Kociuszko Mound's breath-taking panoramic vistas of Krakow and its surrounds are one of its greatest attractions. On clear days, visitors may go to the mound's summit and take in a magnificent view of the city and the adjacent Tatra Mountains.

The Kociuszko Mound Museum is located at the foot of the mound and is devoted to Tadeusz Kociuszko's life and accomplishments. His military exploits and his impact on Polish history are commemorated at the museum via historical artefacts, records, and exhibitions.

Cultural Events: The vicinity of the mound periodically holds cultural events, concerts, and festivals, transforming it into a bustling and active location for both residents and visitors.

Nature and hiking: The Krakus Hill and the surrounding area provide enjoyable options for walking and trekking, giving visitors a chance to see the area's natural splendour.

Krakow's Kociuszko Mound is a major historical site that exemplifies both the city's pride in its national hero and its continuous fight for independence.

A unique opportunity to learn about Polish history, take in breathtaking views of Krakow, and pay respects to a cherished national hero is to visit the Kociuszko Mound. For tourists interested in Poland's rich history and illustrious leaders, it is a place of cultural and historical importance and a must-visit location.

Cruising the Vistula River

The beauty of Krakow and its surrounds may be enjoyed and relaxedly experienced from a new angle on a Vistula River cruise. The longest river in Poland, the Vistula River, also known as Wisa in Polish, passes through numerous significant towns, including Krakow. A Vistula River cruise includes the following significant elements and highlights:

Beautiful views of Krakow's skyline, old bridges, and riverbank sites may be had on a river cruise. It offers a unique chance to take in the city's architecture and surrounding natural beauties from the sea.

Peaceful Ambience: Away from the bustle of the city streets, cruising down the Vistula River offers a quiet and tranquil experience. It enables guests to relax and take in the boat's gently rocking as it travels over the lake.

Historical landmarks: You may find historical landmarks like Wawel Castle, the Kociuszko Mound, and the lovely Kazimierz neighbourhood along the riverbanks. The trip offers a unique viewpoint on these well-known sites.

Sunset cruises are especially well-liked since they provide a wonderful and romantic environment as the sun sets over the river and the city lights come on.

Cruises with Onboard eating: Some river cruises have onboard eating options, enabling passengers to savour delectable meals while taking in the river scenery. This is a wonderful opportunity to enjoy both scenery and delicious cuisine.

Guided Tours: Many river cruises provide educational commentary from experienced tour leaders who share insights into the past and present of Krakow and the Vistula River.

Opportunities for Photography: A river trip offers fantastic chances to take pictures of the city's bridges, monuments, and watery reflections.

Nature & wildlife: Depending on the time of year, you could see a variety of birds and other animals along the riverbanks, which will to the appeal of the trip.

All tourists of all ages may take part in a Vistula River cruise, which is a family-friendly activity. The boat journey and the opportunity to see the city from a new angle are often enjoyed most by children.

Tours that may Be Customised: There are many lengths and themes for river cruises, so guests may choose the one that best fits their schedule and tastes.

An enjoyable and peaceful way to take in Krakow's beauty and charm is on a boat down the Vistula River. Whether you choose a romantic sunset boat or a daytime sightseeing tour to take in the city's monuments, the sensation of gliding down the river will leave you with priceless memories of your trip to Krakow.

The Blue Lagoon at Zakrzówek

Zakrzówek, sometimes known as "The Blue Lagoon," is a well-liked resort town near Krakow, Poland. A magnificent blue lagoon surrounded by towering cliffs and lush vegetation has been created within a disused limestone quarry that has been filled with water. Here are some of Zakrzówek - The Blue Lagoon's salient qualities and highlights:

Natural Beauty: Due to the distinctive geological characteristics of the limestone quarry, Zakrzówek is recognised for its stunningly brilliant blue water. The lagoon is an alluring and gorgeous location for both inhabitants and visitors due to its vivid blue colour.

Crystal clean Water: Because of the Blue Lagoon's extremely clean water, swimming and diving are very popular activities there. Visitors may witness aquatic life and underwater rock formations because to the visibility.

Zakrzówek has grown to be a well-liked diving location in Krakow. Divers get the chance to explore underwater cliffs, caverns, and other fascinating structures in the flooded quarry.

Rock climbing: Rock climbers who are looking for difficult routes and spectacular views of the water below are drawn to the granite cliffs that surround the lagoon.

Recreational Activities: At Zakrzówek, visitors may partake in a number of recreational pursuits, including hiking along the area's beautiful paths, picnics, and sunbathing.

Nature Reserve: The region around Zakrzówek has been declared a nature reserve, offering a protected home for regional wildlife and plants.

Panoramic Views: From the lagoon, visitors may enjoy breathtaking panoramas of the area's nature and, in the distance, the city of Krakow.

Historical Background: The quarry was previously a source of limestone that was utilised to create many of Krakow's ancient structures.

Zakrzówek is a well-liked site for both residents and visitors looking for a natural getaway in Krakow since it is conveniently located from the city centre.

When visiting Zakrzówek, you should take safety precautions, particularly if you want to participate in water sports like diving and swimming.

Zakrzówek - The Blue Lagoon is a hidden treasure in Krakow, providing a unique fusion of unspoiled landscape, fun activities, and a dash of history. Whether you're searching for excitement via diving and rock climbing or a quiet day by the ocean, Zakrzówek offers a rejuvenating and delightful experience for everyone.

CHAPTER (SIX)
Traditional dishes from Poland

Polish food is full of substantial, savoury dishes that pay homage to the nation's culinary heritage and history. Here are a few treasured by both residents and tourists alike classic Polish dishes:

Pierogi: The most well-known Polish cuisine is likely pierogi. Typically, these delectable dumplings are stuffed with a variety of ingredients, including meat, potatoes and cheese, sauerkraut and mushrooms, or sweet cottage cheese. Typically, they are boiled before being topped with melted butter, sour cream, or fried onions.

Bigos: Another name for this classic Polish stew is "Hunter's Stew." It is cooked with fresh cabbage, sauerkraut, and various meats, such as sausages, bacon, and sometimes even game meat. The dish is perfectly slow-cooked, producing a tasty and filling supper.

Urek: Urek is a traditional Polish dish made of sour rye soup. The soup's distinctively acidic flavour comes from the use of fermented rye flour. Boiling potatoes, sausage and hard-boiled eggs are often served with it.

Traditional beetroot soup known as "barszcz" may be consumed either warm or cold. It has a vivid crimson colour and is often served with sour cream or a dollop of smetana, a dairy product that resembles sour cream.

Polish sausages, or kielbasa, are available in a variety of styles and flavours. They may be grilled, boiled, or fried and are created with various meats and seasonings. A popular element in many Polish cuisine is kielbasa.

Kotlet Schabowy: A beloved comfort meal in Poland, kotlet schabowy is a breaded pork cutlet similar to a schnitzel. The usual accompaniments are mashed potatoes and cabbage salad.

Gobki: Gobki, also known as cabbage rolls, are produced by enclosing rice or barley with minced meat (often a mix of beef and pig) between cooked cabbage leaves. Then a tomato-based sauce is added, and they are baked or stewed.

Makowiec: During special events and holidays, a poppy seed roll known as a makowiec is often offered as dessert. Ground poppy seeds, sugar, and sometimes almonds and raisins are used to make the sweet filling, which is then wrapped in a delicate, yeast-based dough.

Racuchy: Racuchy are yeast- or baking-powder-based Polish pancakes. They may be consumed with a variety of toppings, including powdered sugar, jam, or fresh fruit, and are often offered for breakfast or as a dessert.

Traditional Polish cheesecake known as sernik is created with a combination of farmer's cheese (twaróg), eggs, sugar, and is often flavoured with vanilla or lemon zest. For fans of cheesecake, it is a must-try treat.

These are but a few examples of the mouthwatering and reassuring foods that Polish cuisine has to offer. You are certain to taste the cosiness and heartiness of Polish home cuisine whether you sample pierogi, bigos, or any other classic Polish meal.

Best Dining in Krakow

Krakow is recognised for its thriving restaurant scene, which has a variety of eateries that may accommodate different tastes and preferences. Here are some of Krakow's top eateries, chosen for their outstanding cuisine, setting, and overall eating experience:

Pod Aniolami: This Old Town restaurant provides classic Polish food with a contemporary touch. It is housed in a historic edifice. A pleasant environment for savouring traditional Polish meals with a hint of refinement is created by the restaurant's attractive design and attentive service.

Wierzynek: Wierzynek, which dates back to the 14th century, is one of Krakow's oldest and most distinguished restaurants. The restaurant specialises on Polish and European cuisine and provides a quality dining experience. The restaurant is the ideal option for special events due to its illustrious past and opulent setting.

Miod Malina: Miod Malina is a delightful eatery that offers traditional Polish cuisine in a warm and inviting atmosphere. The restaurant is renowned for its handmade pierogi and delectable desserts and offers a range of regional dishes on its menu.

Cyrano de Bergerac: This French-inspired eatery is well-known for its delicious steaks and seafood dishes. It is a great option for a special dining experience due to the exquisite design and professional service.

Szara Ges: Szara Ges is a restaurant serving Polish and foreign cuisine that uses high-quality, regionally produced products. It is situated in the centre of the Main Market Square. The lively plaza is beautifully visible from the restaurant's patio.

Plankton is a restaurant that seafood lovers should not miss. Fresh, regional fish is the main attraction at this cosy seafood restaurant, which also offers meals with Mediterranean and Asian influences.

Chimaera: In Krakow, there is a well-known vegetarian and vegan restaurant called Chimaera. It provides a unique and varied cuisine that includes meals produced with fresh and organic ingredients that are plant-based.

Starka: Starka is a distinctive eatery that specialises in meals prepared with traditional Polish alcoholic beverages, mainly vodka and starka, the aged variation of vodka. The menu offers traditional Polish dishes with a vodka touch, making for a unique and memorable dining experience.

Pod Baranem is a gourmet dining establishment that combines the culinary traditions of Poland and Israel. The restaurant is a standout option for a fine lunch due to its attractive decor and creative food.

Dynia Restobar: A hip restaurant with an emphasis on fresh and locally sourced products, Dynia Restobar combines Polish and foreign flavours. Both residents and tourists are drawn to it by its relaxed and informal vibe.

These eateries are only a few of the many outstanding eating options Krakow has to offer. If you're wanting either traditional Polish food or flavours from across the world, Krakow's eclectic restaurant scene is guaranteed to provide.

Favourite cafes and street fare

Both residents and tourists may enjoy delectable delights and fast snacks at Krakow's excellent array of cafés and street food vendors. Here are some of Krakow's well-liked cafés and food vendors:

Popular cafes

Café Camelot: A beautiful café with a bohemian vibe may be found close to Planty Park. It's a wonderful location for resting in a welcoming environment while consuming coffee, pastries, and small meals.

The unusual café Massolit Books & Café blends a cosy coffee shop with a bookshop. Visitors may have a cup of coffee or a piece of baked cake while perusing literature in different languages.

Café Bunkier: With a lively ambiance and outdoor seating, this establishment can be found close to Planty

Park and the Main Market Square. It's the perfect place to unwind while taking in a variety of drinks and light food.

Café Philo: This quiet retreat from the busy city is hidden away in a courtyard. It is renowned for its top-notch coffee, handcrafted pastries, and variety of vegetarian and vegan alternatives.

Charlotte: A chic café renowned for its art deco decor and delectable coffee. A range of breakfast and lunch options are available at this well-liked brunch location.

Karma Coffee: This speciality coffee establishment is committed to serving coffee that is produced with integrity. For coffee lovers seeking for a superior brew, it is a must-stop.

Fast Food:

Open-faced sandwiches called zapiekanki are constructed with half a baguette and topped with cheese, mushrooms, and other ingredients. Zapiekanki are sold by street sellers all around the city.

Kielbasa: Kielbasa, or sausages, are a common ingredient in Polish street cuisine. Vendors grill a variety of sausages, which are often served on buns with toppings like mustard and sauerkraut.

Obwarzanki: A Krakowian bagel variety, obwarzanki are often topped with salt, sesame seeds, or poppy seeds. They may be found at many street booths and are a well-liked snack dish.

Placki ziemniaczane: These Polish latkes-style potato pancakes. They are served with toppings like sour cream or applesauce after being deep-fried till crispy.

Polish crepes called nalesniki may be filled with savoury or sweet ingredients including cheese, fruit, or mushrooms. From street vendors, they are often served hot.

Polish doughnuts known as pazki are stuffed with cream or jam. They are a delectable sweet delight that may often be found at bakeries and food carts, particularly on holidays like Fat Thursday.

Krakow is a food lover's delight because to the amazing variety of flavours and culinary experiences available in its cafés and street food sellers. Every taste is catered for in Krakow's culinary scene, whether you're in the mood for a leisurely coffee or a fast lunch on the run.

CHAPTER (SEVEN)

Souvenirs and Markets

There are several marketplaces and gift stores in Krakow where tourists may buy one-of-a-kind presents, authentic Polish goods, and keepsakes to cherish. Here are some of Krakow's well-liked marketplaces and places to buy souvenirs:

The old Renaissance Cloth Hall (Sukiennice), which is housed in the Main Market Square, has stores and souvenir vendors. Numerous traditional Polish handicrafts, amber jewellery, works of art, textiles, and other mementos are available here.

St. Florian's Gate Market: A bustling outdoor market with booths offering mementos, artwork, and crafts can be found just outside St. Florian's Gate. The market is a great location to purchase regional goods and presents.

Visit the Christmas Market in Krakow if you're in the city during the holidays. It's located in the Main Market Square. It's a festive market with holiday-themed merchandise, mulled wine, traditional dishes, and Christmas decorations.

Kazimierz Market: In the Kazimierz neighbourhood, a bustling market with booths offering antiques, vintage goods, and one-of-a-kind products can be found. It's a terrific spot to discover unique items and souvenirs that have historical appeal.

Amber Shops: Poland is well-known for its premium amber, and Krakow is home to a large number of amber stores. Beautiful and significant souvenirs may be obtained in the form of amber jewellery, sculptures, and ornamental objects.

Traditional Polish Crafts: Keep an eye out for stores and stands that offer hand-painted pottery, wooden carvings, and folk art, among other traditional Polish crafts. These products are a wonderful way to carry a bit of Polish culture back to your own country.

Gift stores may be found within Wawel Royal Castle and sell a variety of things pertaining to Polish history and aristocracy. The rich history of the castle is well represented in the objects you may discover here.

Polish Food and Spirits: As mementos, don't forget to get some traditional Polish foods and liquors. To share with friends and family, local specialities like vodka, Polish pickles, honey, and traditional sweets make for delectable presents.

Polish Folk Costumes: Polish folk costumes and accessories may be found at various specialised shops and gift shops if you're interested in wearing traditional Polish apparel.

In order to support regional artists and companies, always purchase sensibly and hunt for genuine Polish-made goods. Watch for the "Polskie" mark, which denotes that the product was produced in Poland. The chance to interact with local vendors and learn more about Polish culture and workmanship is another benefit of shopping at markets and small businesses.

Local Goods to Purchase

You may purchase a variety of regional goods in Krakow as gifts or to bring home as a reminder of Poland's rich cultural history. Here are a few well-known local goods to take into account:

Polished amber, sometimes known as "Baltic gold," is renowned for its superb quality and is used in jewellery. Numerous stores and marketplaces have a large selection of amber jewellery, including necklaces, bracelets, earrings, and rings.

Polish pottery is renowned for its vivid colours and elaborate patterns. It is made of hand-painted ceramics. Look for hand-painted ceramic objects with traditional folk designs, such as plates, bowls, mugs, and ornamental items.

Traditional Polish cuisine: To experience the tastes of Poland, bring some traditional Polish cuisine items home. Popular options include Polish sausages (kielbasa), pickles, jams, honey, chocolates, and conventional sweets.

Polish Vodka: Poland has a long history of producing vodka, and there are several high-quality Polish vodka brands available. For memorable presents, look for bottles with distinctive flavours or packaging.

Polish folk art and crafts are a reflection of the nation's voluminous traditions. Unique and significant mementos include things like hand-painted wooden boxes, carved wooden figures, and carefully woven linens.

Polish stoneware, commonly referred to as Bolesawic pottery, is another well-liked ceramic product. Kitchenware with the characteristic blue and white designs is lovely and long-lasting.

Polish specialties: In addition to sausages and pickles, think about purchasing smoked sheep's milk cheese, Krakowian bagels, or traditional cakes and pastries from Poland.

Traditional Polish Costumes: Polish folk costumes and accessories may be found at specialised shops or gift shops if you're interested in wearing traditional Polish attire.

Polish Art and Souvenirs: Look through the stores and art galleries to find creations by regional photographers and painters. Supporting the local creative scene by purchasing local artwork or photographs is a terrific idea.

Polish souvenir T-shirts and postcards are available at tourist stores and market stalls for a reasonable price. They include recognisable Krakow and Polish symbols.

To guarantee authenticity and quality while buying locally produced goods, make an effort to purchase from recognised shops and vendors. To ensure that a product is created in Poland, look for the label "Polskie" (Polish). Haggling is not often accepted in Poland's stores or marketplaces, although you may attempt it at select outdoor markets like the St. Florian's Gate Market. Take pleasure in your shopping and hold onto your Polish trinkets as enduring memories of your trip to Krakow.

Streets and Malls for Shopping

With a mixture of beautiful retail lanes and contemporary malls, Krakow has a varied shopping landscape. The following are a some of Krakow's best retail avenues and centres:

Streets for retail:

Florianska Street: One of Krakow's most well-known and active retail streets is Florianska Street. It connects St. Florian's Gate to the Main Market Square and is lined with a number of retail establishments, boutiques, and gift stores. Along this ancient street, you can buy anything from apparel and accessories to amber jewellery and traditional Polish crafts.

Another well-liked retail route in the Old Town is Grodzka route. It is lined with gift stores, art galleries, and boutiques and extends from Wawel Castle to the Main Market Square.

Kazimierz neighbourhood: Known for its bohemian and artistic vibe, the Kazimierz neighbourhood has a wide variety of specialty stores and boutiques. You may discover antique shops, art galleries, and boutiques providing handcrafted goods and high-end goods here.

Near the Main Market Square, the streets of ul. Szewska and ul. Bracka are well-known for their chic clothing shops and high-end retailers.

ul. Starowislna: This street links the Old Town with the Kazimierz neighbourhood and has a variety of chic cafés, vintage shops, and trendy boutiques.

Shopping Centres:

Galeria Krakowska is one of the biggest and busiest retail centres in Krakow, and it is situated right close to the city's major train station (Krakow Glowny). There are more than 270 retailers there, including national and international chains, fashion boutiques, electronics stores, and a sizable food court.

Galeria Kazimierz is a contemporary retail centre with over 150 stores, eateries, and entertainment options. It is located in the Kazimierz neighbourhood. It provides a variety of fashion, beauty, and home products retailers.

Bonarka City Centre is a large retail centre with more than 200 shops, a movie theatre, and a variety of restaurants and cafés. It is situated in the southern section of the city.

M1 Shopping Centre: Located in Krakow's north, M1 Shopping Centre has a number of stores, a food court, and a play area for children.

The Serenada Shopping Centre is a modest mall outside of Krakow that provides a laid-back shopping experience with a variety of stores and culinary establishments.

Krakow offers a variety of shopping experiences to suit every taste and fashion, whether you choose to browse through contemporary shopping malls with a vast selection of shops or wander through old streets and purchase at quaint boutiques. Enjoy your shopping!

CHAPTER (EIGHT)

The Museum and Memorial at Auschwitz-Birkenau

The sombre and important historical landmark known as the Auschwitz-Birkenau Memorial and Museum honours the victims of the Holocaust and is situated close to the Polish town of Owicim. It is among the most popular Holocaust monuments in the world and was named a UNESCO World Heritage Site in 1979. The Auschwitz-Birkenau Memorial and Museum is described in the following way:

History: During World War II, Nazi Germany built the biggest concentration and extermination camp at Auschwitz-Birkenau. It was in use from 1940 to 1945 and largely used to arrest and kill Jews, as well as other targeted populations such Poles, Romanis, Soviet POWs, and those considered enemies of the Nazi state.

Auschwitz I: The original building of the complex, Auschwitz I, was designed to accommodate political prisoners from Poland. Later, it became into a location for mass murder thanks to the usage of crematoria and gas chambers. Today, Auschwitz I is home to the museum and a variety of exhibits, including artefacts, records, and pictures that serve as a sobering reminder of the horrors of the Holocaust.

Auschwitz II-Birkenau: Built as an extermination camp, Auschwitz II-Birkenau is situated roughly two kilometres from Auschwitz I. There were barracks, gas chambers and crematoria spread out across a vast region. The bulk of Holocaust victims were slaughtered at Birkenau.

Guided Tours: In order to give historical context and guarantee respectful and educational experiences, guided tours are often used for visitors to the Auschwitz-Birkenau Memorial and Museum. Numerous languages are supported, and owing to strong demand, reservations are advised.

Commemoration and Reflection: The memorial site gives visitors the chance to take some time for introspection and to remember the people who perished and suffered there. While visiting, it is crucial to maintain a respectful and sombre attitude.

The Auschwitz-Birkenau Memorial and Museum is very important for teaching people about the Holocaust and the repercussions of prejudice, hatred, and totalitarian ideologies. It acts as a potent reminder of the need to stop such crimes from occurring in the future.

Information for Visitors: Due of its historical importance, visitors should be advised that visiting Auschwitz-Birkenau might be emotionally taxing. It is advised to wear proper attire and comfortable walking shoes, and big bags or backpacks are not permitted within the structures.

Although the experience may be emotionally taxing, many guests feel it to be a profoundly poignant and necessary visit to respect the victims' memories and guarantee that the historical lessons are never forgotten. As a monument to the horrors of the Holocaust and the significance of advancing tolerance, compassion, and human rights, the Auschwitz-Birkenau Memorial and Museum must be approached with respect and understanding.

Salt Mine of Wieliczka

In the town of Wieliczka, close to Krakow, lies one of Poland's most well-known and intriguing tourist destinations: the Wieliczka Salt Mine. It is one of the world's oldest salt mines and has been in use for more than 700 years. An overview of the Wieliczka Salt Mine is provided below:

The Wieliczka Salt Mine, which has a long history dating back to the 13th century, was important to Poland's economics and history. It was a vital component of the nation's salt trade and a major source of wealth for the Polish rulers.

Production of salt: Up until 2007, when it was designated a historical monument, the mine continued to produce salt. Since then, it has mostly served as a tourist destination. It might have generated 30,000 tonnes of salt a year at its height.

Underground Complex: Over the course of many centuries, miners constructed tunnels, chambers, and chapels out of rock salt in the Wieliczka Salt Mine. The mine was included to the UNESCO World Heritage list due to its distinctive architecture and beautiful salt sculptures.

Tourist Attractions: Visitors may enjoy guided tours of the salt mine, which takes them through a variety of chambers and passages. The magnificent salt sculptures, which include chandeliers, statues, and even a complete subterranean church, the well-known St. Kinga's church, may be seen by visitors.

Health Benefits: It is said that the salt mine has health advantages because of its favourable microclimate, which is considered to help those with allergies and respiratory problems. As a consequence, the mine has been divided into areas with therapeutic chambers for tourists looking for treatment from certain ailments.

Salt Lake: The mine has Lake Wessel, an underground salt lake where tourists may ride boats and take in the distinctive ambience of the subterranean environment.

Accessibility: Visitors have a variety of tour choices, including half-day and full-day trips, and the mine is conveniently located from Krakow. Tickets and excursions must be reserved in advance, particularly during the busiest travel seasons.

St. Kinga's Festival: To honour the patron saint of salt miners, a unique festival known as the St. Kinga's Festival is celebrated every year in the Wieliczka Salt Mine.

Experiencing salt mining in Poland's past and learning about its importance via a visit to the Wieliczka Salt Mine is a unique and unforgettable experience. For history buffs and intrepid travellers alike, the mine's subterranean world with its stunning salt sculptures and spectacular chambers is a must-visit location.

The Tatra Mountains and Zakopane

A charming village called Zakopane may be found in southern Poland, tucked away at the base of the Tatra Mountains. Both outdoor enthusiasts and those looking for a pleasant alpine hideaway frequent this location. An overview of Zakopane and the Tatra Mountains is shown below:

Due to its reputation as a winter sports destination, Zakopane is sometimes referred to as the "Winter Capital of Poland". It is also a well-liked destination for summer getaways since it offers breathtaking mountain scenery and a variety of outdoor activities.

Poland and Slovakia are naturally separated by the Tatra Mountains, the highest range of the Carpathian Mountains. In the Polish portion of the Tatras, the Tatra National Park provides an abundance of hiking paths, breath-taking scenery, and a wide variety of species.

Outdoor recreation: Zakopane and the Tatra Mountains are a hiker and nature enthusiast's dream come true. There are pathways for hikers of all skill levels, from leisurely strolls to strenuous climbs to peaks like Giewont and Rysy.

Skiing & Winter Sports: During the winter, Zakopane's well-maintained ski slopes attract skiers and snowboarders. Ski slopes in the surrounding regions, such Kasprowy Wierch and Gubaówka, are available for both novice and expert skiers.

Gubaówka Hill: Gubaówka is a well-known hill close to Zakopane that may be reached by funicular train. Visitors may take in expansive views of the town and the Tatra Mountains from the summit.

Highland tradition: Zakopane is renowned for its distinctive architecture, which mixes old-fashioned wooden buildings with elaborate carvings. The Goral people, a highland ethnic minority renowned for their distinctive rituals and mythology, are strongly ingrained in the town's culture.

The major pedestrian thoroughfare in Zakopane is Krupówki Street, which is packed with stores, eateries, and vendors offering regional crafts, trinkets, and traditional highland fare.

Thermal Pools: After a long day of skiing or climbing, tourists may unwind in one of the local thermal pools, including Terma Bania or Aqua Park Zakopane.

Lake Morskie Oko: Morskie Oko, often known as "Eye of the Sea," is one of the Tatra Mountains' most beautiful lakes. It provides a lovely location for a day excursion and is accessible on foot or by horse-drawn carts.

Take a cable car to the highest accessible mountain in Poland, Kasprowy Wierch, for a breathtaking perspective of the Tatra Mountains.

An attractive location, Zakopane and the Tatra Mountains provide the ideal balance of scenic beauty, outdoor activity, and charming culture. The breathtaking scenery and welcoming people of this mountainous area will enchant you whether you go there for hiking or skiing in the winter.

CHAPTER (NINE)
Krakow transport

Krakow's transport system is well-developed and provides a number of practical choices for navigating the city and its surroundings. The primary transit options in Krakow are as follows:

Trams: Within Krakow, trams are a well-liked and effective mode of transportation. The majority of the city, including the tourist hotspots and city centre, is covered by the city's vast tram network. Trams are a useful way to travel about fast and run often.

Buses: Krakow has a robust bus network that works in conjunction with its tram system. Buses offer links to the city's outside and service places that trams do not traverse. Bus stations are well signposted, and they operate often like trams.

Night buses are also available in Krakow, operating after normal bus and tram service has ended for the evening. For individuals who need to travel beyond normal public transit hours, night buses are available.

Taxis: Taxis may be hailed on the street or reserved using taxi applications, and they are widely accessible throughout Krakow. Use trusted taxi services or ride-hailing apps to guarantee a reasonable charge. Although more costly than public transportation, taxis may still be a practical choice, particularly for late-night travel.

Uber: Uber operates in Krakow and offers a substitute for standard taxis. The ride-hailing service is often a cheap and practical method of getting about the city.

Rental Bikes: The city of Krakow has a system for sharing bicycles called "Wavelo," which provides rental bikes at different locations. Renting a bike is a great way to take advantage of the city's many bike lanes and trails while touring it at your own leisure.

Walking: Krakow's historic city centre is small and simple to navigate on foot. The Old Town's picturesque streets, squares, and attractions are best explored on foot.

Private Cars: Although Krakow has a decent public transportation system, some tourists choose to hire a vehicle for greater freedom, particularly if they want to go beyond the city or explore the nearby locations.

It is important to note that Krakow is a rather pedestrian-friendly city and that many of the main tourist sites are close to one another. However, trams, buses, and cabs are dependable and reasonably priced choices for travelling about Krakow when travelling to destinations beyond the city centre or if public transportation is not available.

Options for Accommodation

Krakow has a variety of lodging choices to fit any traveler's needs and price range. You'll discover a variety of options in various parts of the city, from opulent hotels to affordable hostels. Here are a few of the most well-liked lodging choices in Krakow:

Hotels: Krakow offers a wide choice of lodging alternatives, from boutique inns and budget hotels to opulent five-star establishments. Since there are so many hotels in the city centre, seeing the top sights is simple.

Hostels: Hostels are a popular option for travellers on a tight budget. Numerous hostels in Krakow provide cheap dorm beds and individual rooms. In addition, hostels are a fantastic place to meet other travellers.

Bed and breakfasts and guesthouses: These accommodations provide a more private and intimate setting. They may be found across the city in different neighbourhoods and are often family-run businesses.

Apartments and holiday rentals: If additional room and solitude are important to you, you may choose to rent an apartment or a vacation house. There are many possibilities for short-term stays, and they are especially practical for groups or families.

Apart-hotels: Apart-hotels mix the convenience of an apartment with the luxuries of a hotel. For those who want to make their own meals, they provide studio or apartment-style lodgings with kitchenettes.

Boutique Hotels: Krakow is home to a number of attractive boutique hotels, many of which are housed in old structures and have distinctive décor.

Hostels with Private Rooms: For travellers who want more solitude but still want to experience the hostel environment, several hostels also offer private rooms with en-suite toilets.

Luxury Resorts: Krakow has a number of upscale resorts and spa hotels in the nearby countryside if you're seeking for a nice place to stay.

Agrotourism: If you're looking for a special experience, think about staying at an agrotourism farm in the local countryside. These lodgings provide a glimpse of rural life in Poland and often feature handmade meals.

Think about things like location, facilities, and price when selecting a place to stay. Major attractions and a thriving nightlife are easily accessible if you stay in or close to the city centre. However, more tranquil areas outside the city might provide a more laid-back ambiance. Make sure to reserve your favourite lodging in advance, particularly during the busiest travel times.

Emergency and Safety Contacts

Krakow is typically a secure city for tourists, but like any well-known tourist destination, it's important to take certain security measures to protect yourself. Keep in mind the following safety advice and emergency numbers while visiting Krakow:

Personal Security

Be mindful of your surroundings, particularly at night, and stay away from remote or dimly lighted regions.

Be careful with your things and alert for pickpockets, particularly in busy tourist locations.

For transportation, choose renowned and authorised taxi services or ride-hailing applications.

Don't interact with pushy street salespeople or those who appear unduly persistent.

Emergency numbers:

Call the 112 emergency hotline in Europe in case of an emergency. For police, medical, and fire situations, dial this number.

You may call the neighbourhood police directly at 997 if you need non-emergency help or to report a crime.

Tourists may get advice at the Krakow Tourist Information Centre and learn about a variety of amenities and activities. Call them at +48 12 421 77 87 or stop by their location at 52 Main Market Square to speak with them.

Healthcare and Health:

You may call an ambulance if you need medical attention by dialling 999 or 112.

Having travel insurance that provides coverage for medical situations is advised.

Krakow has a large number of pharmacies, several of which are open late or around-the-clock. For a pharmacy, look for the green cross symbol.

Drinking alcohol:

Be careful while taking beverages from strangers, particularly in regions with a lot of nightlife.

Alcohol use in public places is prohibited in Poland, with the exception of venues like beer gardens and events with permits.

Safer public transport:

In general, Krakow's public transit is secure, but you should still be cautious with your things, particularly during rush hour or on packed trams and buses.

Change of Currencies:

Use authorised currency exchange locations or ATMs to make cash withdrawals. Avoid exchanging money with currency dealers on the street.

Foreigners who Need Emergency Medical Assistance:

There are specialised medical facilities for tourists for international visitors who want medical care. One such institution that offers medical services to overseas patients is the International Health Centre at 1 W. Azarza Street.

You may have a safe and pleasurable trip to Krakow by being cautious and adopting the necessary safety measures. Keep in mind to safeguard your critical papers (such as your passport, visa, and ID) and carry a copy of your emergency contact information at all times. Enjoy your time here in this lovely city!

Useful Polish Phrases

When travelling to Krakow or any other place where Polish is spoken, learning a few simple words in the language may be useful and welcomed. Here are some sentences to help you get going:

1. Good day - Cze (cheshch)
2. Dzie dobry (dzyen doh-bri) means good morning.
3. Greetings and good afternoon (dzyen doh-bri)
4. Salutations: Dobry wieczór Dobri Vyeh Choor
5. Do widzenia (doh vee-dzen-ya) means "goodbye."
6. Prosz (pro-sheh), please.
7. Thank you, please. (jen-koo-yeh)
8. Tak (tahk) affirms.
9. No, please (nyeh)
10. Please pardon me/excuse me - Przepraszam (pshe-prah-sham)
11. What does this cost? Is that costly? (Ee-leh to Koo-too-yeh?)
12. Where is that? Where is it at...? "(gdzyeh yest)"
13. Nie rozumiem (nyeh ro-zoo-m'yem) means I don't comprehend.
14. Can you assist me? Can you help me, please? Chi Mo Zhe Mee Po Mots
15. To your health, cheers! A happy ending! (nah zdrov)
16. Are you an English speaker? - Do you speak English? Chi Moo Vish Poh An Gyel School
17. Tell me your name. How are you on imi? Yak mash na im-yem
18. "Mam na imi" (mam na im-yem) is how I introduce myself.

19. In which loo are you? Where is the Azienka? (dzyeh yest wah-zeen-ka?

Please give me the bill. Poprosz rachunek, please. Pop-ro-sheh Rah-hoo-nek

Your encounters with locals will be more fun and demonstrate your respect for their language and culture if you learn and use these words. If your Polish pronunciation isn't flawless, don't be disheartened; most Poles will appreciate your attempt to speak to them in their language.

Printed in Great Britain
by Amazon

35916888R00056